POLISH JEWS

A PICTORIAL RECORD

ROMAN VISHNIAC

—

POLISH JEWS

A PICTORIAL RECORD

WITH AN INTRODUCTORY ESSAY
BY ABRAHAM JOSHUA HESCHEL

SCHOCKEN BOOKS · NEW YORK

First SCHOCKEN PAPERBACK edition 1965

10 9 8 7   84 85 86

In 1938, on the eve of the Second World War, Roman Vishniac traveled from the Baltic Sea to the Carpathian Mountains, photographing the Jewish communities of Eastern Europe. The Jews of Eastern Europe — we call them "Polish Jews" in our title, for reasons of cultural (not physical) geography — were at that time only a year distant from catastrophe. The collection of photographs that Roman Vishniac brought back constitute the last pictorial record of the life and character of these people.

From this wealth of material, thirty-one photographs were selected for this book, not merely because of their aesthetic value, but because they make up together one great portrait of a life abjectly poor in its material condition, and in its spiritual condition, exaltedly religious.

In 1938, on the eve of the Second World War, Roman Vishniac traveled from the Baltic Sea to the Carpathian Mountains, photographing the Jewish communities of Eastern Europe. The Jews of Eastern Europe — we call them "Polish Jews" in our title, for reasons of cultural (not physical) geography — were at that time only a year distant from catastrophe. The collection of photographs that Roman Vishniac brought back constitute the last pictorial record of the life and character of these people.

From this wealth of material, thirty-one photographs were selected for this book, not merely because of their aesthetic value, but because they make up together one great portrait of a life abjectly poor in its material condition, and in its spiritual condition, exaltedly religious.

THE culture of the Sephardic Jews of the Iberian peninsula marked a brilliant epoch in Jewish history, distinguished not only by monumental scientific achievements but also by the universality of its spirit.

In Eastern Europe, the spiritual life of the Jews was lived in solitude. Growing out of its own ancient roots and developed in its indigenous environment, their life remained independent of the trends and conventions of the surrounding world. Unique were their cultural patterns in thinking and writing, unique their communal and individual ways of life. Tenaciously adhering to their own traditions, they were bent upon the cultivation of what was most their own, to the utter disregard of the outside world. Literature for them was writing by Jews and for Jews. They did not apologize to anyone, nor did they compare themselves with anyone else.

In Eastern Europe the Jewish people had come into its own. It did not live like a guest in somebody else's house, who must constantly keep in mind the ways and customs of his host. The Jews lived in their own way, without reservation and without disguise, outside their homes no less than within them. When they said in their commentaries on the Talmud that "the world asks," they did not refer to a problem raised by Aristotle or a medieval philosopher. The "world" to them was the students of the Torah.

Among the Spanish Jews there were numerous men who possessed high learning. Their achievements in medicine, mathematics, and astronomy contributed greatly to the development and progress of European civilization. Through their translations of scientific and philosophical works from Arabic into Latin they made available to the European nations the treasures of culture and science then in the custody of the Arab world. Many Sephardic authors wrote largely in Arabic; even works dealing with questions of Jewish ritual, homilies on the Bible, and commentaries on the Talmud were often written in Arabic.

To an East-European author it would seem inconceivable to write in a foreign tongue. Unlike the aristocratic society of the Sephardic world, whose poets wrote in a Hebrew so complicated and involved that only erudites could enjoy it, Jewish society in Poland had an intimate, organic character. The healthy earthiness of the villagers, the warmth of plain people, and the spiritual simplicity of the Maggidim penetrated into the house of study and prayer. Laborers, peasants, porters, artisans, they were all partners in the Torah.

The amalgamation of Torah and Israel was here accomplished. Ideals became folkways; the people itself was the source of Judaism, a source of spirit. The most distant became very intimate, very dear. Spontaneously, without external cause, the people improvised customs of religious significance.

Classical books were not written in Eastern Europe. The Talmud, the Mishneh Torah, the Book of Splendor, the Guide of the Perplexed, and the Tree of Life were produced in other countries. East-European Jewry lacked the ambition to create consummate, definitive, perfect expressions. Their books were so rooted in a self-contained world that they are less accessible to moderns than the books of the Sephardic authors. They are not literature, they read like notes of discussions with pupils. They did not write books that stand like separate buildings with foundations of their own; all their works lean upon older books, are commentaries on classical works of ancient time, modestly hug the monumental walls of old citadels of learning.

In their lives everything was fixed according to a certain pattern, nothing was casual, nothing was left to chance. But they also had sufficient vitality constantly to modify the accepted pattern. New customs were continually added to, and the old customs enriched with fresh nuances. The forms and ceremonies were passed on from generation to generation, but the meaning which was attached to them did not remain the same. A perennial source gave renewed life to tradition.

There was profound sadness in their joy. The "moralistic" melodies that the wedding players intoned before the veiling ceremony would almost rend the soul of the bride. Under the canopy, mother and grandmother would sob, and even a man who heard a piece of good news would usually burst into tears.

But the Jews all sang: a student over the Talmud, the tailor while sewing a pair of trousers, the cobbler while mending a pair of shoes, and the preacher while delivering a sermon. A unique form of musical expression evolved.

The dishes to be served on certain days, the manner of putting on or removing one's shoes, the position of one's head when walking in the street — everything was keyed to a certain style. Every part of the liturgy, every prayer, every hymn had its own tune. Every detail possessed its own physiognomy, each object its own individual stamp. Even the landscape became Jewish. In the month of Elul (September), during the penitential season, the fish in the streams trembled; on Lag b'Omer, the scholar's festival in the spring, all the trees rejoiced. When a holiday came, even horses and dogs felt it. And a crow perched on a branch looked from a distance "as though it were wearing a white prayer shawl, with dark blue stripes in front: and it sways and bends as it prays, and lowers its head in intense supplication."

In almost every Jewish home, even in the humblest and poorest, stood a bookcase full of volumes; proud and stately folio-tomes together with shy small-sized books. Books were neither an asylum for the frustrated nor a means for occasional edification. They were furnaces of living strength, time-proof receptacles for the eternally valid coins of spirit. Almost every Jew gave of his time to learning, either in private study, or by joining one of the societies established for the purpose of studying the Talmud or some other branch of rabbinic literature. To some people it was impossible to pray without first having been refreshed by spending some time in the sublime atmosphere of Torah. Others, after the morning prayer, would spend an hour with their books, before starting to work. At nightfall, almost everyone would leave the tumult and bustle of everyday life to study in the Bet ha-Midrash. The Jews did not feel themselves to be the "People of the Book." They did not feel that they possessed the book, just as one does not feel that one possesses life. The book, the Torah, was their essence, just as they, the Jews, were the essence of the Torah.

A Jewish township in Lithuania and in many other parts of Eastern Europe was, in the words of Mendele, "a place where Torah has been studied from time immemorial; where practically all the inhabitants are scholars; where the synagogue or the house of study is full of people of all classes busily engaged in studies, townsfolk as well as young men from afar; where at dusk, between twilight and evening prayers, artisans and other simple folk gather around the tables to listen to a discourse on the great books of Law, to interpretations of Scripture, to readings from theological and ethical writings . . . where on the Sabbath and the holidays, near the Holy Ark, at the reading stand, fiery sermons are spoken that kindle the hearts of the Jewish people with love for the Divine Presence, sermons that are seasoned with words of comfort from the prophets, with the wise parables and keen aphorisms of the sages, in a voice that heartens one's soul, that melts all limbs, that penetrates the whole being."

To be sure, in the life of the East-European Jews there was not only light but also shadow — one-sidedness of learning, neglect of manners, provincialism. In the crowded conditions in which they lived — persecuted and tormented by ruthless laws, intimidated by drunken land-owners, despised by newly-enriched city-dwellers, trampled by police boots, chosen as scapegoats by political demagogues — the rope of self-discipline sometimes snapped. In addition, naked misery and frightful poverty deafened the demands and admonitions of religious enthusiasm. The regions of piety were at times too lofty for plain mortals. Not all Jews could devote themselves to the Torah and service to God, not all the old men had the faces of prophets; there were not only Hasidim and Kabbalists, but also yokels, shnorrers, and tramps.

There were many who lived in appalling poverty, many who were pinched by never-ending worries, and there were plenty of taverns with strong spirits. But drunkards were never seen among Jews. When night came and a man wanted to while away his time, he did not hurry to take a drink; he went rather to his books, or joined a group that, either with or without a teacher, gave itself over to the pure enjoyment of study. Physically worn out by their day's toil, they sat over open volumes and intoned the austere music of the Talmud.

Poor Jews, whose children knew only the taste (as one of their songs has it) of "potatoes on Sunday, potatoes on Monday, potatoes on Tuesday," sat there like intellectual princes. They possessed whole treasuries of thought — the knowledge, ideas, and sayings of many ages. When a problem came up, there was immediately a crowd of people to offer opinions, proofs, quotations. One raised a question on a difficult passage in Maimonides' work, and many vied in attempts to explain it, outdoing one another in the subtlety of dialectic distinctions. The stomachs were empty, the homes overcrowded — but the minds were replete with the riches of the Torah.

A story is told of a simple, uneducated Jew who on the Feast of the Rejoicing of the Torah danced so passionately with the scrolls as if there were no limit to his joy. "Why are you so happy?" someone asked him. "It is natural that scholars who all year round do nothing but search in the Torah should rejoice on this day, but why are you so jubilant?" Answered he: "When my relative celebrates a wedding, do not I have a good time at his feast?"

The state did not have to compel the Jews to send their children to school. Their most popular lullaby proclaimed: "The Torah is the highest good," and mothers at the cradle crooned: "My little child, close your eyes; if God will, you'll be a rabbi." At the birth of a baby, the school children would come and chant the Shema Yisrael in unison around the cradle. When taken for the first time to the Heder, the child was wrapped, like a scroll, in a prayer-shawl. Schoolboys were referred to as "the holy flock," and a mother's tenderest pet name for a boy was "my little zaddik," my little saint. Parents were ready to sell the pillow from under their heads to pay tuition for their children; a poorly tutored father wanted at least his children to be scholars. Women toiled day and night to enable their husbands to devote themselves to study. Those who could not devote themselves to the Torah because of economic exigencies tried at least to support the students. They shared their scanty food with wandering students. And when the melancholy, sweet chanting of a talmudic study coming from the

10

Bet ha-Midrash penetrated the neighboring streets, exhausted Jews on their cots felt sweet delight at the thought that by their acts of support they had a share in that learning. The ambition of every Jew was to have a scholar as a son-in-law, and a man versed in the Torah could easily marry a well-to-do girl and obtain *kest*, board, for a few years, or even permanently, which meant he was able to devote his time to study.

A blazing passion permeated all intellectual activities. It is an untold, perhaps incommunicable story of how mind and heart could merge into one. Immersed in complicated legal discussions, they could at the same time feel the anguish of the Divine Presence that abides in exile. In endeavoring to unravel some perplexity raised by a seventeenth-century commentary on a commentary on the Talmud, they were able in the same breath to throb with sympathy for Israel and all afflicted people. Study was a technique for sublimating feeling into thought, for transposing dreams into syllogisms, for expressing grief in difficult theoretical formulations, and joy by finding a solution to a difficult passage in Maimonides. Tension of the soul found an outlet in contriving clever, almost insolvable, riddles. In inventing new logical devices to explain the word of God, they thrilled with yearning after the Holy. To contrive an answer to gnawing doubts was the highest joy. Indeed, there was a whole world of subdued gayety and sober frolic in the playful subtleties of their *pilpul*.

Their conscious aim, of course, was not to indulge in self-expression — they were far from being intent upon exploiting the Torah — but humbly to partake of spiritual beauty. Carried away by the mellow, melting chant of Talmud-reading, one's mind soared high in the pure realm of thought, away from this world of facts and worries, away from the boundaries of here and now, to a region where the Divine Presence listens to what Jews create in the study of His word. There was holiness in their acumen, the cry, "My soul thirsteth for God, the living God," sounded in their wrestling with the Law.

Their learning was essentially non-utilitarian, generally free of direct and practical designs, an esthetic experience. They delved into those parts of the lore that had no relevance to daily life no less eagerly than into those that had a direct bearing on it. They grappled with problems absent from our mundane reality, remote from the banalities of the normal course of living. He who studied for the purpose of becoming a rabbi was the object of ridicule. In the eyes of these people, knowledge was not a means for achieving power but a way of arriving at the source of all reality.

The *pilpul* was a continuation of the ways of study pursued at the ancient academies in Babylonia in the first centuries of the present era. The goal was not to acquire information about the Law but rather to examine its implications and presuppositions. The method of study was not just to absorb and to remember, but to discuss and to expand. All later doctrines were considered tributaries of the ancient, never-failing stream of tradition. One could debate with the great sages of bygone days. There was no barrier between the past and the present. If disagreement was discovered between a view held by Rabbi Akiba Eiger of Posen, who lived in the nineteenth century, and Rabbi Yizhak Alfassi of Morocco, who lived in the eleventh century, a Warsaw scholar of the twentieth century would intervene to prove that the views were consistent after all, and so the unity of the tradition was maintained.

Just as their thinking was distinguished by a reaching out for the most subtle, so their mode of expression, particularly that of those engaged in mystic lore, was marked by a tendency toward terseness. Their sayings are pointed, aiming at reaching an idea in one bound, instead of approaching it gradually and slowly. They offered the conclusion and omitted the premises. They spoke briefly, sharply, quickly, and directly; they understood each other in a hint.

Audacious doctrines were disguised as allegories, or even witty maxims, and a seeming commonplace often contained a sublime thought. Holy men seemed to be discussing the building of a roof; they spoke of bricks and shingles, while they were actually debating the mysteries of the Torah. Whole theories of life were implied in simple stories told at tea after the *havdalah* ceremony that marked the end of the Sabbath. The power of such *pilpul* penetrated even into the Kabbalah. The later Ashkenazic Kabbalists constructed symbolic labyrinths out of mystic signs; so involved were these labyrinths that only Kabbalists endowed with both mystic passion and intellectual keenness could safely venture into them.

The author of the Revealer of the Deeply Hidden, written in the seventeenth century, interprets in two hundred and fifty-two different ways the portion of the Pentateuch in which Moses pleads with God for permission to enter the Promised Land. The manifest became occult. Everywhere they found cryptic meaning. Even in the part of the Code dealing with civil and criminal law they discovered profound mysteries. Allusions were found in names of towns and countries, as in the name of Poland, which was said to derive from the two Hebrew words, *Po-lin*, "here abide," and to have been inscribed on a note fallen from heaven and found by the refugees from Germany on their eastward journey at the time of the Black Death. On the leaves of the trees, the story goes, are inscribed sacred names, and in the branches are hidden errant souls seeking deliverance through the intermediation of a pious Jew, who in passing would stop to say his twilight prayer under the tree.

In the eyes of these Jews, the world was not a derelict the Creator had abandoned to chance. Life to them was not merely an opportunity for indulgence, but a mission that God entrusted to every individual. Life is at least as responsible an enterprise as the management of a factory. Every man constantly produces thoughts, words, deeds. He supplies these products to the Powers of holiness or the Powers of impurity; he is constantly engaged either in building or in destroying.

Man's task is to restore what has been impaired in the cosmos. Therefore, the Jew is engaged in the service of God. He is rarely dominated by a desire for austere rigorism or a liking for irrational discipline for its own sake. In the main, he is borne up by a sense of the importance of his mission, by the certainty that the world could not exist without the Torah. This sense lends his life the quality of an art whose medium is neither stone nor bronze, but the mystic substance of the universe.

Scientists dedicate their lives to the study of the habits of beetles or the properties of shrubs. Every trifle is significant because it indicates the most intricate qualities of things. The pious Ashkenazic scholars investigated just as passionately the laws that should govern human conduct. They wished to banish chaos from human existence and to civilize the life of man according to the Torah. They trembled over every move, every breath; no detail was treated lightly — everything was serious. Just as the self-sacrificing devotion of the scientist seems torture to the libertine, so the poetry of rigorism jars on the cynic. He does not realize that the question of what benediction to pronounce upon a certain type of food becomes so important because it solves the problem of matching the material with the spiritual. To the uninspired, the Shulhan Arukh is a volume of symphonies whose musical notation they cannot read; to the pious Jew, its signs are full of rhythms and melodies.

In the eighteenth century, the hasidic movement arose and brought heaven down to earth. The Hasidim banished melancholy from the soul and uncovered the ineffable delight of being a Jew. God is not only the creator of earth and heaven, He is also the one "who created delight and joy." He who does not taste paradise in the performance of a precept in this world will not feel the taste of paradise in the other world. "A Jew who does not rejoice in the fact of his being a Jew," said one of the great hasidic teachers, "is ungrateful to heaven it is a sign that he has failed to grasp the meaning of the daily blessing over his not having been born a heathen." Judaism was as though reborn. The Baal Shem rejuvenated us by a thousand years. A new prohibition was added: "Thou shalt not be old!" and the Jews began to feel life-everlasting in a sacred melody, the Sabbath became the vivid anticipation of the life to come.

Jews ceased to fear the flesh. Do not inflict pain upon it, do not torment it — one should pity the flesh. "Hide not thyself from thine own flesh." One can serve God even with the body, even with the evil inclination; one must only be able to distinguish between the dross and the gold. When a little of the other world is mingled with it, this world acquires flavor. Only without nobility is the flesh full of darkness. The Hasidim have always maintained that the joys of this world are not the highest to which one can achieve, and they found in themselves the passion for spirituality, the yearning for the joys of the world to come.

The perception of the spiritual, the experience of the wonder, become common. Plain men begin to feel what scholars have often failed to sense. The sigh of the contrite heart, a little inwardness, or a bit of self-sacrifice outweighed the merits of him who is stuffed with both erudition and pride. When learning is practiced for its own sake, it may become a kind of idolatry. Excessive *pilpul* may dry up the well of the soul. For that reason renowned scholars sometimes close their Talmud volumes and set out to wander in a self-imposed "exile," far from home, among strangers, to bear humiliation and taste the cup of privation and misery.

There is the story of a scholar who came to visit a rebbe. The scholar was no longer a young man — he was close to thirty — but he had never before visited a rebbe.

"What have you done all your life?" the rebbe asked him.

"I have gone through the whole of the Talmud three times," answered the scholar.

"Yes, but what of the Talmud has gone through you?" the rebbe replied.

Man is no mere reflection of the above; he is a source of light. If he divests himself of the husks, he can illuminate the world. God has instilled in man something of Himself. Israel, in particular, because it lives for the "fulfilment of the Torah," is of unique importance. Hence it is that the fate of His beloved people of Israel is of such concern to God. God is the infinite, "the Hidden of all Hidden," whom no thought can conceive; but when a Jew has almost exhausted his strength in yearning after Him, he would exclaim: "Sweet Father!" It is incumbent upon us to obey our Father in heaven, but God in turn is bound to take pity on His children. And His compassion is abundant indeed. "I wish I could love the saintliest man in Israel as the Lord loves the most wicked in Israel," prayed Rabbi Aaron, the Great.

Jews had always known piety and Sabbath holiness. The new thing in Eastern Europe was that something of the Sabbath was infused into the everyday, into weekdays. One could relish the taste of eternal life in the fleeting moment. In such an environment it was not difficult to believe in the *Neshamah yeterah*, the Additional Soul that every Jew is given for the day of the Sabbath. Jews did not build magnificent synagogues; they built bridges leading from the heart to God.

The present moment overflowed its bounds. People lived not chronologically, but in a fusion of the dimensions of time: they lived with the great men of the past, not only in narrating tales about them, but also in their emotions and dreams. Jews studying the Talmud felt a kinship with its sages. Elijah the Prophet, it was believed, attended circumcision ceremonies, and the spirit of the Holy Guests visited their huts on the days of the Sukkot. The past never died in their lives. Among such Jews there lived the Thirty-six Saints who remain unknown to the people and whose holiness sustains the universe. In their souls simple Jews were always prepared to welcome the Messiah. If Isaiah the Prophet were to rise from his grave and were to enter the home of a Jew even on a plain Wednesday, the two would have understood each other.

Korets, Karlin, Bratzlav, Lubavich, Ger, Lublin — hundreds of little towns were like holy books. Each place was a pattern, an aspect, a way in Jewishness. When a Jew mentioned the name of a town like Medzhibozh or Berdytshev, it was as though he mentioned a divine mystery. Holiness had become so real and so concrete that it was perceptible like beauty.

"Why do you go to see the rebbe?" someone asked an eminent scholar who, although his time was precious, would trudge for days to visit his rebbe on the Sabbath.

"To stand near him and watch him lace his shoes," he answered.

When Hasidim were gathered together, they told each other how the rebbe opened the door, how he tasted his food at the table.

What need was there to discuss faith? How was it possible not to feel the presence of God in the world? How could one fail to see that the whole earth is full of His glory? To preach to these Jews the necessity of observing the six hundred and thirteen commandments would have been superfluous. To live in accordance with the Shulhan Arukh had become second nature. To the Jews this was not enough. A leader of the Musar movement once remarked: "If I thought that I should always remain what I am, I would lay hands on myself. But if I did not hope to be like the Gaon of Vilna, I should not be even what I am."

Outwardly they may have looked plagued by the misery and humiliation in which they lived, but inwardly they bore the rich sorrow of the world and the noble vision of redemption for all men and all beings. For man is not alone in the world. "Despair does not exist at all," said Rabbi Nahman of Bratzlav, a hasidic leader. "Do not fear, dear child, God is with you, in you, around you. Even in the Nethermost Pit one can try to come closer to God." The word "bad" never came to their lips. Disasters did not frighten them. "You can take everything from me — the pillow from under my head, my house — but you cannot take God from my heart."

Miracles no longer startled anyone, and it was no surprise to discover among one's contemporaries a man who attained contact with the Holy Spirit. People ceased to think that their generation was inferior to the earlier; they no longer considered themselves epigones. On the contrary, there were Hasidim who believed that it was easier to receive inspiration from the Holy Spirit in their own day than it had been in the early days of the Talmud. For holiness flows from two sources — from the Temple in Jerusalem and from the Complete Redemption in the time of the Messiah. And we are closer to the time of Redemption than the talmudic sages were to the era of the Temple. The light of the Messiah can already be seen before us, illumining contemporary holy men. "One has to be blind not to see the light of the Messiah," were the words of Rabbi Pinhas of Korets.

The feeling prevailed that man was superior to the angels. The angel knows no self-sacrifice, does not have to overcome obstacles, has no free choice in his actions. Moreover, the nature of the angel is stationary, keeping forever the rank in which he was created. Man, however, is a wayfarer; he always moves either upward or downward; he cannot remain in one place. Man is not only the crown of creation, he can become a participant in the act of creation. The Hasidim realize the wide range of their responsibility, they know that entire worlds wait to be redeemed from imperfection. Not only are we in need of heaven, but heaven needs us as well.

In the days of Moses the Jews had a revelation of God; in the days of the Baal Shem, God had a revelation of Israel. Suddenly there was revealed a holiness in Jewish life that had accumulated in the course of many generations. Ultimately, the "We will do and we will listen," is as important as the "I am the Lord thy God"; and "Who is like unto Thy people, like Israel, a nation one in the earth" is as meaningful to Him as "The Lord is One" is to Israel.

The little Jewish communities in Eastern Europe were like sacred texts opened before the eyes of God. So close were our houses of worship to Mount Sinai. In the humble wooden synagogues, looking as if they were deliberately closing themselves off from the world, the Jews purified the souls that God had given them and perfected their likeness to God. There arose in them an infinite world of inwardness, a "Torah within the Heart," beside the written and oral Torah. Even plain men were like artists who knew how to fill weekday hours with mystic beauty.

It was no accident that the Jews of Eastern Europe did away with worldly education. They resisted the stream that threatened to engulf the small province of Jewishness. They did not despise science; they believed, however, that a bit of nobility is a thousand times more valuable than all the secular sciences, that praying every day, "My God, guard my tongue from evil," is more important than the study of physics, that meditating upon the Psalms fills man with more compassion than the study of Roman history. They put no trust in the secular world. They believed that the existence of the world was not conditioned on museums and libraries, but on houses of worship and study. To them, the house of study was not important because the world needed it; on the contrary, the world was important because houses of study existed in it. To them, life without the Torah and without piety was chaos, and a man who lived without these was looked upon with a sense of fear. They realized quite well that the world was full of ordeals and dangers, that it contained Cain's jealousy of Abel, and the evil cruelty of Sodom, but they also knew that there was in it the charity of Abraham and the tenderness of Rachel. Harassed and oppressed, they carried, deep within their hearts, a contempt for the "world," with its power and glory, with its bustling and boasting. Jews who at midnight lamented the glory of God that is in exile and spent their days peddling were not insulted by the scorn of their enemies or impressed by their praises. They knew the world and did not turn it into an idol. The so-called progress did not deceive them, and the magic of the twentieth century did not blind them. They knew that the Jews were in exile, that the world was unredeemed. Their life was oriented to the spiritual, and they could therefore ignore its external aspects. Outwardly a Jew might have been a pauper, but inwardly he felt like a prince, a kin to the King of Kings. Unconquerable freedom was in the Jew, who, when wrapped in tallit and tefillin, consecrated his soul to the sanctification of the Holy Name.

Has there ever been more light in the souls of the Jews in the last thousand years? Could it have been more beautiful in Safed or in Worms, in Cordoba or Pumbeditha?

The present generation still holds the keys to the treasure. If we do not uncover the wealth, the keys will go down to the grave with us, and the storehouse of the generations will remain locked forever.

When Nebuchadnezzar destroyed Jerusalem and set fire to the Temple, our forefathers did not forget the Revelation on Mount Sinai and the words of the prophets. Today the world knows that what transpired on the soil of Palestine was sacred history, from which mankind draws inspiration. A day will come when the hidden light of the East-European period will be revealed.

ABRAHAM J. HESCHEL

ENTRANCE TO THE OLD GHETTO

COURTYARD

OLD JEW

THREE HASIDIM

HASID IN FURRED HAT

SYNAGOGUE COURT

GRANDFATHER AND GRANDDAUGHTER

STOREKEEPER AND CUSTOMER

STOREKEEPER

FISH SELLER

TAX COLLECTOR AND STALL-KEEPER

[WARSAW]

SELLING HORSE-RADISHES

12

STOREKEEPER WITH NOTHING TO SELL

[WARSAW]

PETITIONER

HEDER

THE STUDENT BODY

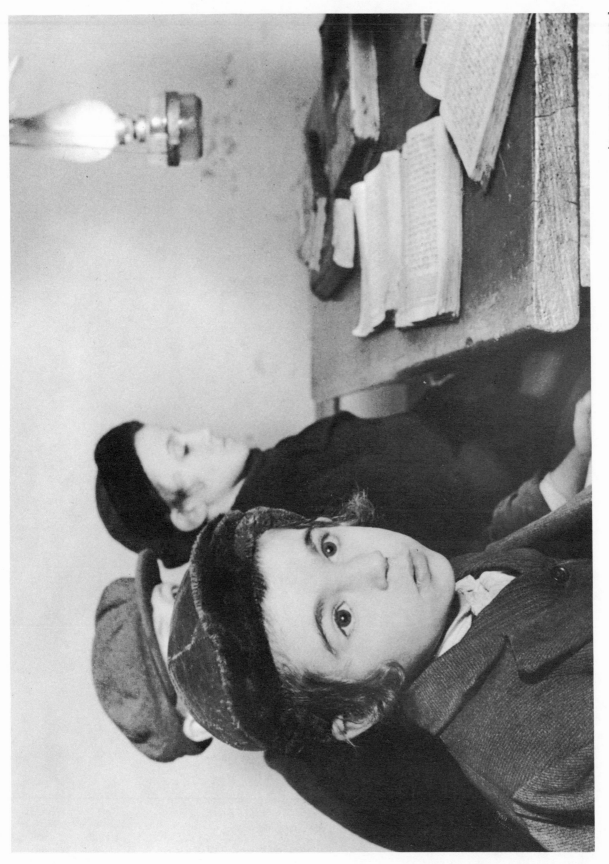

BOYS AND BOOKS

YESHIVA STUDENT

STUDY

[CARPATHIAN RUTHENIA]

EXEGESIS

THE CHANT

[WARSAW]

HALAKHAH

YESHIVA EXAMINATION

[CARPATHIAN RUTHENIA]

BET MIDRASH LIBRARY

RABBIS AND DISCIPLES

[POLAND]

BOY WITH EARLOCKS

26

MAN STUDYING

[CARPATHIAN RUTHENIA]

HASIDIC RABBI

OLD WOMAN

[CARPATHIAN RUTHENIA]

OLD MAN

נפטר י"ג אב תקפ"ט ל'

פנ איש נבון וחכם
תם וישר וירא אלקים
והגה תורת ה' לילות וימי'
זקן ושבע ימים ה"ה
איש צדיק תמים הרבני
מ' ברוך יעקב בן מו"ה
אברהם שלמה ז"ל

[LUBLIN]

GRAVESTONE WITH DETAIL OF BOOKS

31

The introductory essay by Dr. Abraham J. Heschel is part of an address delivered at the Nineteenth Conference of the Yiddish Scientific Institute of New York, by whose permission the present version is printed.